QUESTIONS AND ANSWERS ABOUT ANCIENT HISTORY

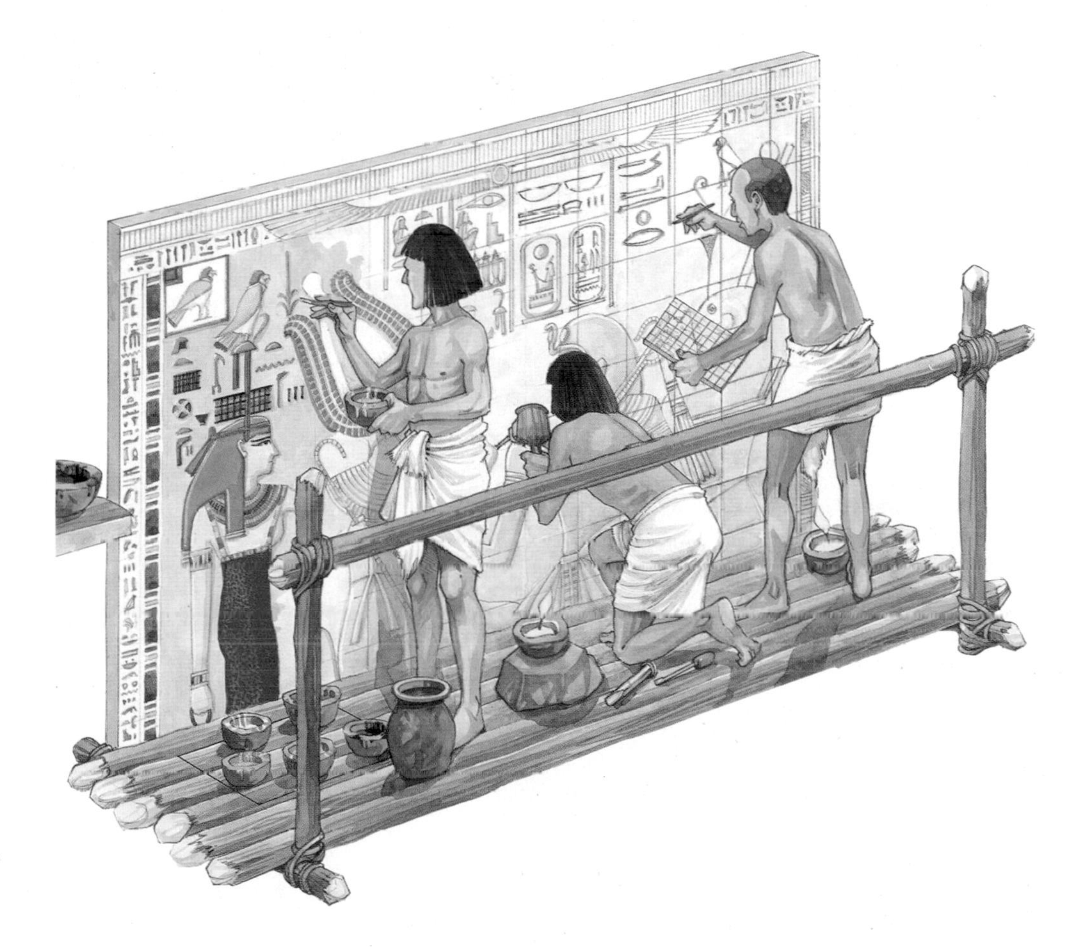

Capella

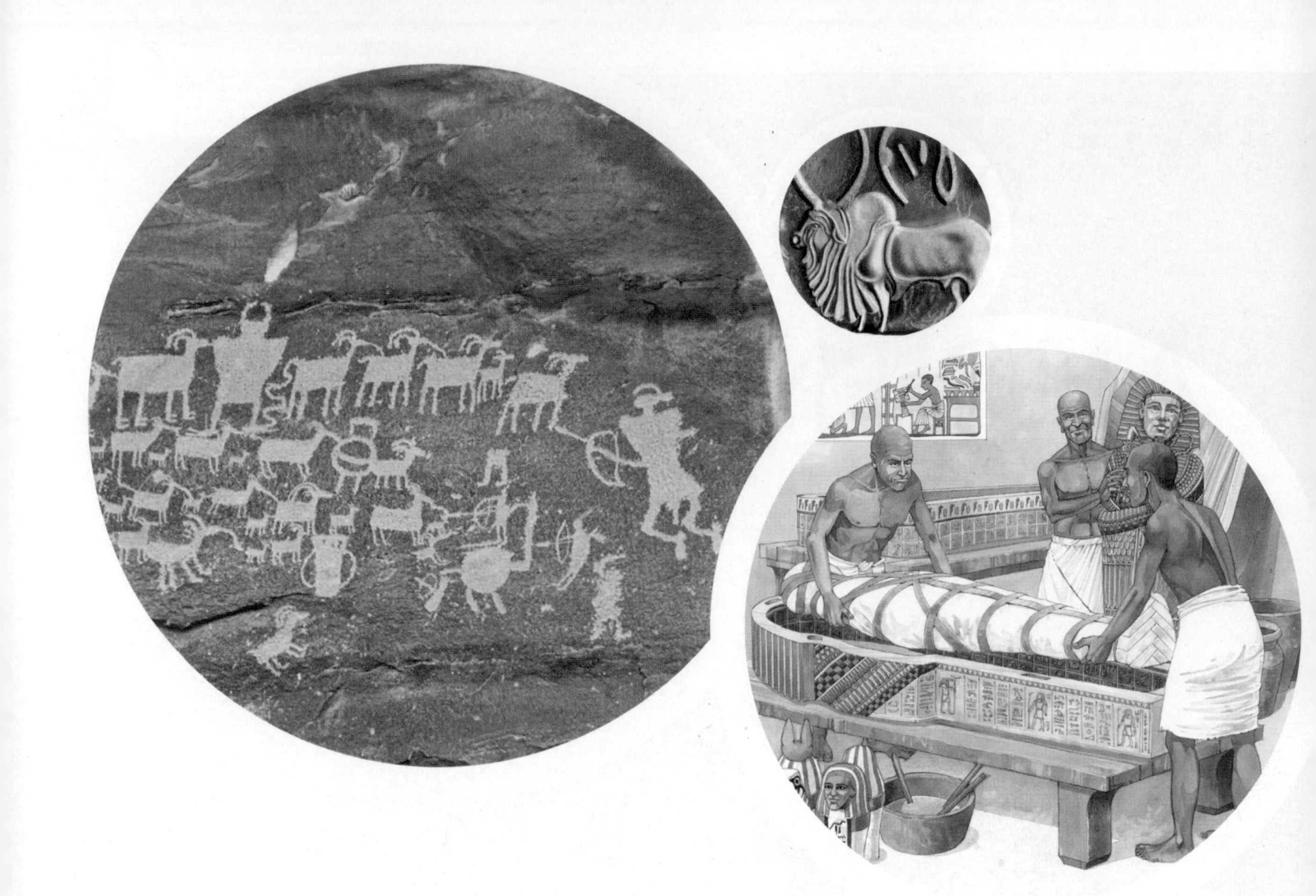

This edition published in 2008 by Arcturus Publishing Limited,
26/27 Bickels Yard, 151-153 Bermondsey Street,
London SE1 3HA

ISBN 978-1-84837-156-9

Designers: Q2A India and Jane Hawkins
Editors: Ella Fern, Fiona Tulloch and Alex Woolf

Printed in China

Contents

Introduction	7
Ancient Mesopotamia	8
Ancient Egypt	9
Ancient India and China	10
Ancient Greece	12
Ancient Rome	14
Ancient Americas	16
Native Americans	17
Medieval Europe	20
Medieval China and Japan	22
Mughal India	24
Incas and Aztecs	25
Architecture	26
Art and Artists	27
World Religions	28
Index	30

Introduction

This book covers a period of around six and a half thousand years, from the earliest civilizations in Mesopotamia in about 5000 BC to the end of the medieval period in about AD 1500. During that period, primitive farming communities grew into powerful and warlike civilizations. Humans learned to built spectacular and lasting monuments, from the Colosseum in Rome to the Great Wall of China. Artists created objects of lasting beauty—Egyptian wall paintings, Greek urns and Ming vases.

In this book, you will learn about the classical civilizations of Europe, as well as the rich cultures of Asia and the Americas. You will discover many fascinating facts about human history in the ancient and medieval periods. When were the first Olympic Games held? Which early American civilization discovered chocolate? Did King Arthur exist? And who built the Taj Mahal as a tomb for his beloved wife? You will find the answers to these and many other questions in the pages of this book.

Ancient Mesopotamia

A large part of ancient Mesopotamia is now covered by the country of Iraq. The fertile land near the Euphrates and Tigris rivers is known as the "Cradle of Civilization," and it was here that the first ever Mesopotamian civilizations were born. Mesopotamia was home to the ancient cultures of the Sumerians, Akkadians, Babylonians and Assyrians.

▲ **Symbols of the past**
The cuneiform is the oldest script in the world.

Quick Q's:

1. Which was the oldest Mesopotamian civilization?

The Sumerians settled in Mesopotamia about 4000 BC, making them the first civilization in the world.

2. Who ruled Mesopotamia?

Every Mesopotamian city was ruled by a king, who was thought to have been chosen by the god of the city.

3. Were there wars in ancient Mesopotamia?

Mesopotamians fought with each other over land, water and power. The first ever war probably took place between the cities of Lagash and Umma.

Q What did the Mesopotamians do for a living?

A A large part of the Mesopotamian society consisted of farmers. The Sumerians were the world's first farmers. They cultivated a variety of crops including wheat, barley and flax. The climate in Mesopotamia was dry, so the people living there had to depend on the rivers for irrigation. They built canals to carry water from the rivers into large reservoirs, where it was stored. The farmers also built dykes to protect their houses from floods.

Q Why did the Mesopotamians build boats?

A Apart from farming, Mesopotamians also traded in goods like stone and metal. They realized that these materials could be transported easily along the rivers and across the sea using boats. So the Mesopotamians built different types of boats. They had wooden boats with triangular sails, a wooden raft called a *kalakku,* and a tub-like boat made of reeds and covered with animal skin known as a *guffa.*

Q What is a *ziggurat?*

A The Mesopotamians believed that their cities and towns were protected by gods. They built temples to these gods on top of large, pyramid-like structures called *ziggurats.* These were made of mud bricks and had between three and seven storeys. The ziggurat was often built at the center of the city.

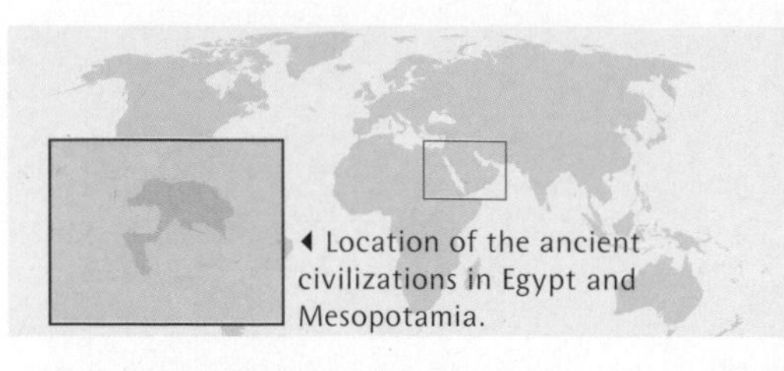

◀ Location of the ancient civilizations in Egypt and Mesopotamia.

▼ **Watering the land**
Mesopotamians were very clever. They built elaborate canals and dams to irrigate their dry farm lands.

▲ **Down the river**
Boats were used for transport and trading goods in ancient Mesopotamia.

Q Were the Mesopotamians really the first people to develop writing?

A The Sumerians were the first to develop a written language. Their script is known as cuneiform and was composed of a series of symbols. These were carved on to clay tablets using a reed called a stylus. They used the tablets to keep records of trade and land ownership. There were some religious texts too. The Sumerian script was adapted by later civilizations, including the Akkadians.

Ancient Egypt

The civilization of ancient Egypt on the banks of the Nile lasted for more than 3,000 years and was the longest continuous civilization in the world. During this period there were many political and economic changes, but the basic culture, religion and lifestyle remained the same throughout.

Q Why is the Nile River known as the lifeline of Egypt?

A It was the fertile banks of the Nile that attracted early settlers to Egypt. These settlers formed two different kingdoms—Upper Egypt in the south, and Lower Egypt in the north, with the Nile Delta. People fished in the Nile and farmed on its banks.

Q Why did ancient Egyptians build pyramids?

A Ancient Egyptians built pyramids as a final resting place for their kings, called pharaohs. They believed that their pharaohs continued to look after the affairs of the kingdom even after death. It was therefore necessary to make their souls comfortable. The Great Pyramid of Khufu, made out of stone, is the grandest of all pyramids. This amazing monument is over 146 meters (480 feet) tall and has survived for more than 4,000 years!

Q What is a mummy?

A The ancient Egyptians believed in life after death. They thought that each person had three souls—*ka*, *ba* and *akh*. It was said that the body had to remain intact even after death for *akh* to exist happily. So, the ancient Egyptians preserved dead bodies by a process called embalming. The process was known only to some priests. The embalmed body is called a mummy, and some have survived until today!

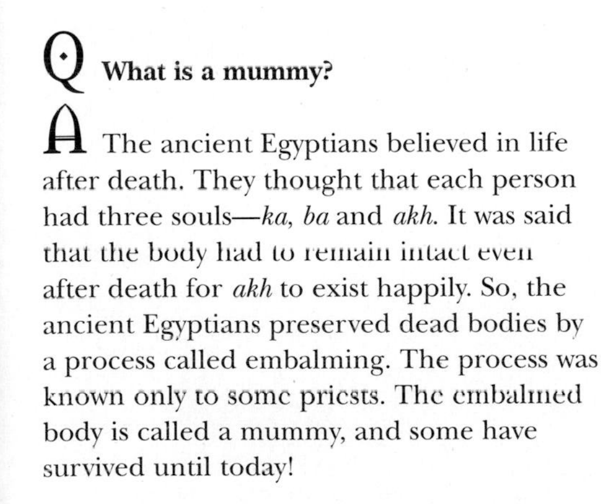

Deciphering sacred carvings

The ancient Egyptians used a form of writing that was made up of pictures. This was known as hieroglyphics. The word hieroglyphic means sacred carving in Greek. For years, no one could read these strange-looking symbols. Then, in 1799, the famous Rosetta Stone was discovered at Rashid (Rosetta), in Egypt. This stone contains an order issued by the priests of Ptolemy V in 196 BC. The order is written in a mixture of Egyptian hieroglyphics, Greek and other ancient scripts. With the help of the Greek texts, experts were soon able to decipher the hieroglyphic script.

▲ **Massive effort**
Many people were needed to build a pyramid.

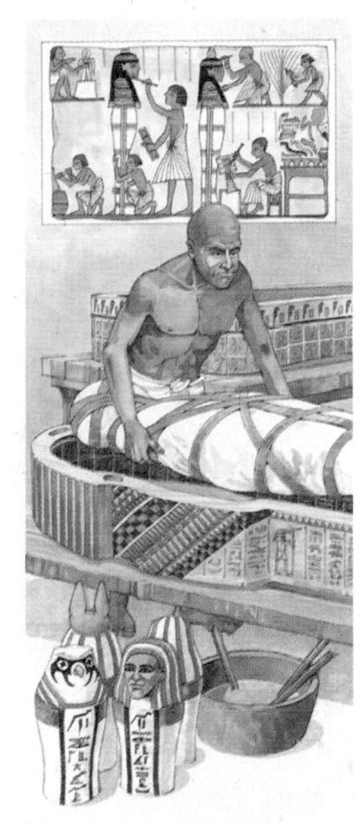

▲ **Comfortable afterlife**
Ancient Egyptians buried food, furniture, jewelry and everything else that was thought necessary for the afterlife along with the mummies. It was believed that the dead had to be well-provided for if they were to perform their duties effectively after death.

Try these too...

Architecture (26),
Art and Artists (27),
World Religions (28–29)

Ancient India and China

Most ancient civilizations developed in river valleys. The Indus Valley civilization, from 3000 to 1500 BC, covered Afghanistan, Pakistan and western India. The Chinese civilization developed along the banks of the Hwang-ho River in about 2100 BC and was governed by various dynasties, or ruling families.

▲ Unknown script
A seal of the Indus Valley civilization, with its unknown script.

Quick Q's:

1. What is Mohenjo-Daro?

Mohenjo-Daro was the largest city in the Indus Valley and means mound of the dead. It had been abandoned for many centuries. Then in 1924, while a railway line was under construction, workers started digging near the mound. When archeologists saw the ancient bricks the workers were digging up, they realized they had hit upon an important ancient site.

2. Who was Empress Xi Ling-Shi?

Empress Xi Ling-Shi is said to have discovered silk when a cocoon fell into her cup of tea and the silk unraveled. By 3000 BC, silk was worn by Chinese royalty.

Q What was special about the ancient Indus Valley civilization?

A The Indus Valley civilization grew up around 3000 BC along the banks of the Indus and Ghaggar-Hakra rivers. Before this, people generally lived in the forest or in small villages. When the civilization developed, great cities were built, with populations of up to 35,000 people. These cities were very advanced and carefully planned with straight roads. The people knew how to make baked bricks out of mud and they built homes two storeys high. Each home had a well and a bathroom from which waste drained in to sewers through clay pipes, some of which were covered and were high enough for a man to walk through. The sewers drained in to a river or the sea.

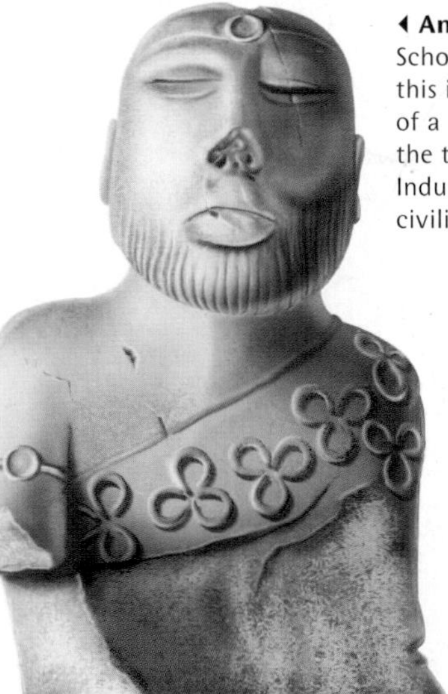

◄ Ancient priest
Scholars think this is the statue of a priest from the time of the Indus Valley civilization.

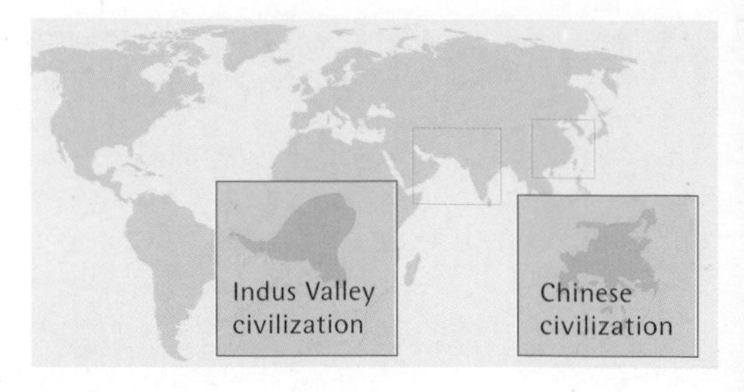

Q What did the people of the Indus Valley do for a living and for recreation?

A Farmers grew barley, peas, melons, wheat, cotton and dates, and herdsmen kept sheep, pigs, cows and water buffalo. Fishermen caught fish using hooks like modern fishermen do today. Grain was stored in a large town granary. Specialized writers kept records of trade and land ownership on the terracota seals. The people were expert artists and potters, and could weave. They could work metal to make jewelry, statuettes and weapons. There were market days every week, to which people came from far away. Colorful clothes and jewelry were sold in the markets. The women wore lipstick made out of vegetable dyes. The men went hunting, sometimes with falcons. Children played with different toys like small carts, whistles shaped like birds, and monkeys that slid down a string.

▼ Swimming pool or religious bath?
The great bath of Mohenjo-Daro may have been used for ritual bathing before prayers. But some scholars think it was also used for recreation.

Q What are the early Chinese dynasties known for?

A The Xia dynasty is the earliest known Chinese dynasty (2100–1600 BC). It lasted for about fourteen generations. During the Shang dynasty (1600–1027 BC), a written language began to take shape and history started to be recorded. At this time, people also learned to make things out of bronze.

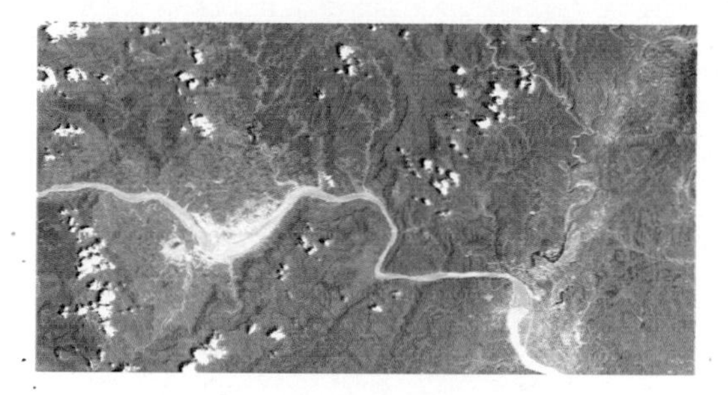

◂ River valley
An aerial view of part of the Yangtze river and its valley, where the ancient Chinese civilization was developed over many centuries.

The Shang dynasty in China was followed by the Zhou dynasty (1027–221 BC), when the Chinese learned to use iron. The rulers of this period encouraged their people to grow crops, spin silk, make pottery, build boats and carts, and hunt with bows and arrows. In 221 BC, Emperor Qin Shi Huang became the first king to rule over the whole of China. He made sure that all Chinese people spoke the Qin language. A written language with over 3,000 characters was developed.

Q Who was Confucius?

A Confucius was born in 551 BC during the rule of the Eastern Zhou dynasty. He was a teacher and a philosopher. He traveled widely, giving advice to different rulers and trying to convince them to be more caring toward their people. He believed in the family and in peace, truth and cooperation. He also believed that the king should be just and fair. The years of Confucius are known as the Golden Age of Chinese philosophy. His teachings were followed by generations of rulers and officials who governed China.

Teatime

The ancient Chinese knew all about tea. Tea, which they called *tu*, was grown in China from at least 1000 BC. It was often used in religious ceremonies. For a long time, the leaves were eaten like vegetables. Gradually, from the time of the Western Han dynasty around 207 BC, people began to use tea as a medicine and as a royal drink. But it wasn't until the Tang dynasty, which began in 618 AD, that drinking tea became an important part of Chinese life.

▾ Destroying knowledge
Emperor Qin Shi Huang ordered the burning of most books in the country in 213 BC, destroying very valuable information about ancient China. He believed that those who wrote books were spreading dissent against him.

Try these too...

Medieval China and Japan (22–23), Mughal India (24), Architecture (26), Art and Artists (27), World Religions (28–29)

Ancient Greece

The ancient Greek civilization is the oldest in the Western world. This civilization thrived about 3,000 years ago. One of the earliest cultures to flourish in the Greek islands was the Minoan civilization on the island of Crete, which began around 2700 BC. The ancient Greek civilization we know today emerged around 800 BC.

◂ Location of the ancient Greek civilization.

Quick Q's:

1. Did ancient Greeks know about democracy?

Democracy—a form of government elected by the citizens of a country—was first introduced in Athens.

2. Who was Homer?

Homer is one of the best-known Greek writers. He wrote the two famous epic poems—*The Iliad* and *The Odyssey*.

3. What is the Parthenon?

The Parthenon is the most famous building of ancient Greece. It was a temple to Athena, the Greek goddess of war and wisdom. The Parthenon has been renovated many times. The latest round started in 1975, and has been going on since then.

4. Did ancient Greeks make pottery?

Ancient Greeks made pottery for their daily use. Some of the most commonly used vessels included amphora (wine jars), hydria (water jars) and krater (mixing bowls). These vessels were often painted with beautiful scenes from famous Greek legends.

Q What are city-states?

A Ancient Greece was divided into many small, self-governing communities. This was largely because of the geography of Greece, where every island and many cities are cut off from their neighbors by mountain ranges or sea. These small, independent communities formed what were known as city-states. Each city-state had its own customs and laws. The most important city-states were Athens, Sparta, Corinth and Thebes.

▴ **Pottery class**
Ancient Greeks had a system of training in all the arts.

Q What caused the Peloponnesian War?

A Around the fifth century BC, the Athenians became very powerful. They began to dominate all the other city-states, especially in war.

The city of Sparta became jealous and, supported by Corinth, went to war against Athens in 431 BC. The Peloponnesian War lasted for 27 years. Athens was defeated. It was stripped of its navy and lost its colonies.

Q Were ancient Greeks good at art?

A The Statue of Zeus at Olympia by Phidias was one of the seven wonders of the ancient world. The statues made in ancient Greece showed detailed knowledge of the human anatomy. Ancient Greek architecture consisted mainly of temples. They had simple square or rectangular shapes, surrounded by tall columns. Greek art has had enormous influence on the cultures of many countries.

◂ **War**
The ancient Greeks were well-known for the many wars they fought on land and sea. City-states fought one another, then united to fight Persian invaders.

Q What did the ancient Greeks do for fun?

A Ancient Greeks enjoyed watching plays. Almost every city had open-air theaters where drama festivals took place. Awards were given to the best playwright. Greek tragedy and comedy have had a lasting impact on Western drama and culture.

Q When were the first Olympic Games held?

A The ancient Greeks were keen sportsmen. The Olympic Games were an athletic and religious celebration held in the town of Olympia. The first Olympic Games were held in 776 BC, in an attempt to bring all the city-states together in friendly competition.

Q Did girls in ancient Greece go to school?

A Only boys went to school in ancient Greece. Girls were not sent to school. They were taught housework and married by the age of 13. Women were not allowed to go out to work, or even to vote. Only men took part in the affairs of the state.

Birth of democracy
In the city-states of ancient Greece, men openly debated and voted on many issues.

Ancient Olympics
A discus thrower takes part in a competition in ancient Greece.

Try these too...

Ancient Rome (14–15), Medieval Europe (20–21), Architecture (26), Art and Artists (27)

Living in slavery

Slaves in ancient Greece had no rights at all—they didn't even have their own names! They used the names their masters gave them. People became slaves in many ways; some were children of slaves, some were abandoned as infants; some were children sold by their families for money. Prisoners of war also became slaves.

Ancient Rome

The ancient Roman civilization was the most powerful of all ancient civilizations. In the beginning Rome was a small city-state that was under the control of the Etruscans. It soon grew to become the largest empire in the ancient world. Ancient Rome was greatly influenced by the ancient Greek culture.

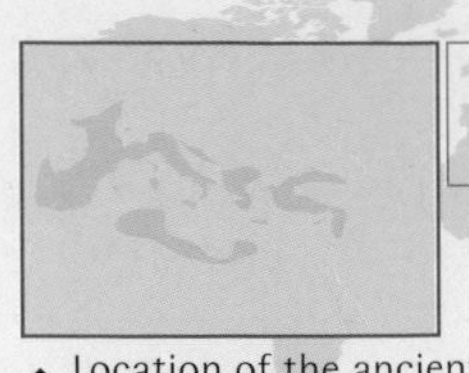

▲ Location of the ancient Roman civilization.

Quick Q's:

1. What was special about the Colosseum?

The Colosseum is a huge open-air theater in Rome. It was built by Emperor Vespasian and his sons. It held 50,000 people. Gladiatorial games and mock naval battles were the main events held in it.

2. Did all ancient Romans wear togas?

A toga was a long piece of cloth worn by men in ancient Rome. It was usually draped over the tunic. The toga was a symbol of the person's position in society. Therefore, slaves and most poor men did not wear togas.

3. What are *insulae?*

The poor people in ancient Rome lived in small, crowded apartments known as *insulae.* These apartments had only 2–3 rooms, and large families lived in them.

4. Who were the *bestiarii?*

Sometimes, criminals who had been sentenced to death and prisoners of war were forced to fight wild animals with their bare hands in the Roman arena. They were called *bestiarii.*

Q When was Rome founded?

A According to legend, Rome was founded on 21 April 753 BC by Romulus and Remus, who were twins born to Mars, the Roman god of war. A fight broke out between the two brothers regarding the exact location of the city of Rome, and Romulus ended up killing Remus. Romulus then finished building the city that was later named Rome after him.

Q Was ancient Rome ruled by kings?

A Romulus was the first of the Seven Kings of Rome to rule the city. Around 509 BC, Tarquin, the last of the Seven Kings, was made to step down from the throne and the Roman Republic was established. Under this system, Rome was ruled by magistrates and other representatives who were elected by the people. The Republic of Rome dominated all of western Europe. However, by 30 BC, Rome once again came under the rule of kings and became known as the Roman Empire. The Roman Empire was later divided into two parts—eastern and western.

▲ **Roman soldiers**
Roman soldiers were the best trained, the most disciplined and the most feared in the ancient world.

Q Who were the Five Good Emperors?

A The Five Good Emperors ruled ancient Rome between AD 96 and 180. They were Nerva, Trajan, Hadrian, Antoninus Pius and Marcus Aurelius. The Five Good Emperors were so-called because ancient Rome prospered the most under them. They were known for their fair policies and good rule.

◀ **Army officer**
An army officer was an important citizen in Rome, especially during the time the Roman Empire was expanding. They held titles that showed the number of soldiers they commanded. For example, a centurion commanded a hundred soldiers.

Q Were the ancient Romans good at engineering?

A Ancient Romans were brilliant architects and engineers who constructed magnificent buildings throughout the Empire. However, they are best known for their amazing public baths, roads, aqueducts and drainage systems. Baths were a very important part of life in ancient Rome. Both men and women visited the baths at least once a day. The water in the baths was channeled through aqueducts.

▲ **Roman bath**
The Roman bath had many rooms, with water at various temperatures and facilities for exercise.

Q Why did ancient Romans build aqueducts?

A The Romans built aqueducts to carry water to the cities. Sometimes, the water would be carried from rivers or streams as far as 95 kilometers (59 miles) away! They used natural gravity to carry the water over such long distances. Wherever there was a depression, walls or arches were built over it to keep the water flowing. The water was stored in a large tank, or *castellum*, in the city, from where it was distributed to public fountains and baths.

▲ **Roman banquet**
Roman banquets went on for hours.

Q What did ancient Romans do for recreation?

A Ancient Romans loved dance and music. The rich held elaborate feasts in which they served exotic food like oysters, pork and snails and entertained their guests. All the people were very fond of gladiatorial games.

Try these too...

Ancient Greece (12–13), Architecture (26), Art and Artists (27)

▼ **The scribe**
The scribe was an important part of ancient Rome. He wrote down all the laws and the debates in the senate.

Paving the way

Apart from baths and aqueducts, ancient Romans also built roads, some of which still exist today. Roads in ancient Rome had multiple layers. The bottom layer, was made of mortar. This was covered with a layer of stones and cement. Next, a layer of concrete and slabs of stone was added to this. Finally, the upper layer of concrete and smooth pebbles was laid. This method of building roads is known as paving.

Ancient Americas

Middle America, also called Mesoamerica, is the region that stretches from central Mexico to northern Honduras. In ancient times, it was home to some highly developed civilizations like the Maya and the Olmec. These civilizations prospered until the arrival of the European settlers in the sixteenth century.

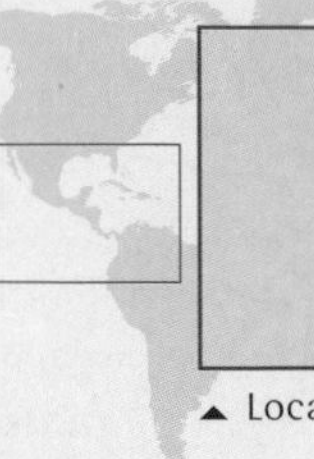
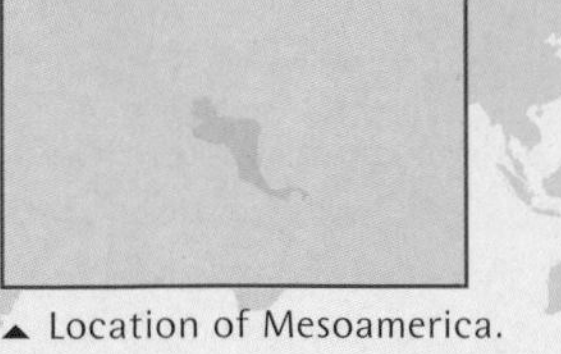

▲ Location of Mesoamerica.

Quick Q's:

1. What type of gods did Mesoamericans believe in?

Ancient Mesoamerican gods were part human and part animal. They represented natural elements like the Sun and the Moon, rain, lightning and the various planets.

2. Who discovered the cocoa that we all love?

The Maya loved to drink hot cocoa. They believed cocoa was a gift from their snake god Quetzalcoatl and that it could cure them of illness. Chocolate is made from cocoa.

3. Why did the Mesoamericans bury jewelry with their dead?

The Mesoamericans believed in life after death. They buried their dead with jewelry, vases and toys they thought were needed in the afterlife. The Mayans believed that ordinary people went to the underworld when dead, but when kings died, they went to heaven and were reborn as kings in another world. When rich people died, they were buried under their own homes, while kings had elaborate tombs.

Q How did the various civilizations in Mesoamerica develop?

A Farming in Mesoamerica goes back to 5000 BC. Various tribes knew each other and traded in food, animal skins and jewelry. Sometimes their armies raided each other's villages. Gradually, large cities with big palaces, temples and flat-roofed pyramids were built for the rich. The rulers were also the priests. The workers grew crops, built houses for the rich and fought as soldiers.

Q Besides farming, what were the other kinds of work in Mesoamerica?

A People wove cloth and made rope, baskets and fishing nets. Traders took their wares to other villages. Huge temples, pyramids and tombs were built. Artisans carved and painted designs on their walls.

▼ **Stepped pyramid**
The huge stepped pyramid built by the Maya at Chichen Itza (Mexico).

Q Who were the Olmec?

A The Olmec were the first group of people to arrive and settle in Central America. They made the area their home by 1200 BC. They had a calendar and calculated time by studying the stars and a written language which they engraved on stone. Later civilizations learned many things from them, such as how to build houses. This is why they are the mother culture of Mesoamerica.

▲ **Big heads**
Enormous statues of helmeted heads are the best-known examples of Olmec art. Some were 3 meters (10 feet) tall.

Q Why are the Maya special?

A The Maya took the study of astronomy and mathematics much further than the Olmecs had done. They built huge observatories to study stars. They were excellent artists and built grand structures like palaces and ceremonial platforms. They made tools and weapons from volcanic glass.

Native Americans

People have lived in North America for more than 12,500 years, since before the end of the last Ice Age. Scholars believe that these people moved from Asia to America through the Bering Land Bridge during the last Ice Age.

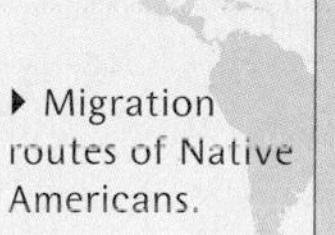

▸ Migration routes of Native Americans.

Q Where did these people come from?

A Most people believe that the early Americans crossed the Bering Land Bridge from central Asia. This bridge now lies underwater. Gradually people spread out across North America. The people of different regions developed different ways of life.

Q Who were the Mississippians?

A The Mississippians were hunter-gatherers who lived in the south-eastern part of what is now the United States. They began to grow crops about 5,000 years ago. About 2,400 years ago, they learned how to grow maize crops. They also grew beans, squash and sunflowers. They buried their dead under huge mounds. They knew how to bake pottery and they built four-walled homes of clay and thatch. Some of them lived in a city called Cahokia.

▾ **Warrior**
Native American warriors often dressed to look like the animals with which they felt a spiritual bond.

Q Did people live in other parts of North America?

A The Delaware, Mohegans, Mohawks and Abenaki lived in the north-east of America. They were good hunters and used spears, bows and arrows and clubs. They fished with spears, hooks and nets and lit flares to attract fish to the surface. They knew how to make two types of homes—the longhouse covered with bark and the wigwam covered with reeds and animal skins.

Try these too...

Incas and Aztecs (25), Art and Artists (27)

◂ **Classic teepee**
Native Americans in the Great Plains designed a wigwam that could be put up and dismantled very quickly.

The story of Hiawatha

The Iroquois people were constantly fighting among themselves. After the death of his family a heartbroken chief, Hiawatha, was wandering in the forest when he met the Peacemaker, who helped him to overcome his grief. The Peacemaker took Hiawatha and visited all the Iroquois tribes and convinced them to live in peace. The tribes got together to form the Iroquois Confederacy. This Confederacy continues and is one of the oldest political groups in North America, far older than the government of the United States.

▲ **God of fertility**
Kokopelli is a fertility god who was worshiped by Native Americans in the south-western part of the United States.

Quick Q's:

1. Why are Native Americans also called American Indians?

Columbus believed he had landed in India when he reached America. He called the locals Indians.

2. Why did their population fall?

Europeans carried diseases which the native Americans had not known. They were unable to fight smallpox, measles, bubonic plague, cholera, typhoid fever, scarlet fever, pleurisy, mumps, diphtheria, pneumonia, whooping cough, malaria and yellow fever. Some groups were wiped out.

3. Were they prepared for Europeans?

Battles with the better-armed Europeans killed many Native Americans. As the Europeans wanted more land, the tribes were pushed back. Many could not adjust to their new homes and died.

Q Who were the Apache Indians?

A The deserts of what is now the south-western United States were occupied by nomadic hunter-gatherers and farmers. The people who lived here included the Apache and Navajo. The farmers grew maize, squash and beans. They often lived in pueblos, or terraced stone and adobe brick homes built around a square. They were good farmers who could grow enough crops in a dry place to support entire villages. Each clan had a headman. Most Apache lived in a *wickiup*, a hut shaped like a dome or a cone of grass and reed mats over a frame. Each wickiup had a fire pit and a smoke hole. Navajo lived in cone or dome-shaped *hogans*, which had six or eight sides. The doors of hogans always faced east. A hogan was almost a sacred place since the Navajo believed the roof symbolized Father Sky and the floor was Mother Earth.

Q Why did the Navajo paint sand?

A The Navajo made beautiful sand paintings depicting their gods as part of a healing ceremony. The paintings were done with colored powder made from grinding stones and other objects they found around them. They used five shades: white, black, red, yellow and blue. The colors were dribbled on to sand. The sand painters were guided by the Navajo priests, called shamans. The paintings were done at dawn and wiped out at the end of the day.

▸ **The shaman**
Native American priests, called shamans, were often the local doctors as well.

▲ **Cave dwellings**
The cave dwellings of Mesa Verde (Colorado) in which the Pueblo lived in the twelfth and thirteenth centuries.

Q Were the Native Americans religious?

A Religion was an important part of daily life for Native Americans. Priests called shamans practiced medicine and performed rituals. There were rituals for planting and harvesting. The Green Corn Ceremony was a Cherokee thanksgiving festival. Nothing was taken for granted. Most Native Americans were forgiving people and pardoned all crime except murder. The Navajo believed in ghosts, who they thought were the spirits of their ancestors.

Q Who are the Inuit?

A Inuit means "the people." The Inuit people settled in the Arctic zone in the extreme north of America. These people, who probably migrated to America from central Asia, adjusted well to the extreme cold conditions. Since they could grow little food, they became expert hunters. They also became experts at building igloos, houses made with blocks of ice.

Q How did the Inuit hunt?

A For fishing, the Inuit learned how to use a harpoon, or a spear with a strong line attached to it, that could be hauled back from the water. They also fished with hooks, lines, or spears with three prongs. In summer, they dug out roots and berries, the only plant food in their diet. For meat, they ate whales, walruses, polar bears and musk oxen. They often ate meat raw, since there was little fuel to cook with. The Inuit trained packs of dogs to work for them, pulling their sledges and helping them to hunt. They used the skins of the animals they hunted to make kayak boats, sleds, tools, clothes and even homes. The Central Inuit group or the Caribou Inuit, only hunted land animals and caught freshwater fish.

▲ **An Inuksuk**
An Inuksuk is a direction marker used by the Inuit.

▲ **Newspaper Rock**
On Newspaper Rock in Utah (USA), people have been recording their activities on stone for 2,000 years.

Q Who is the Kennewick man?

A In 1996, the skeleton of a man was found on the shores of the Columbia River near Kennewick, in the state of Washington, USA. Radiocarbon dating showed that the Kennewick man was at least 8,500 years old. His is one of the earliest human skeletons to have been found in North America. Five Native American tribes, led by the Umatilla of the Columbia River Basin, have argued that scientists have no right to disturb the dead. They want the Kennewick man to be buried once again.

▼ **A new monument**
The Crazy Horse Memorial, a mountain monument being built in South Dakota to honor Native Americans.

Frozen home

For centuries, the Central Inuit people have lived in a igloos or snow homes. The igloo was made of blocks of ice laid in a circle like a dome. The ice bricks were covered with soft snow to keep out the freezing wind. Stale air went out through a hole at the top. The people inside could look out through a window made of clear ice. The bed was a platform of ice on which the residents piled fur sheets. People could enter and leave through a covered passage. Most igloos had a smaller room for storage. What most of us do not know is that the igloo was just the winter home of the Inuit. In summer, they lived in tents made of caribou hide and in huts made of earth and grass.

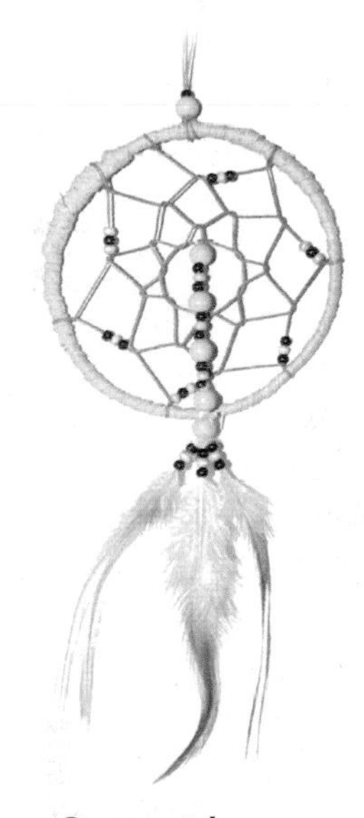

▲ **Dreamcatcher**
The dreamcatcher is a cultural object among many Native Americans. It has a willow hoop and a net, decorated in different ways. There was a belief that it would protect children from nightmares.

Try these too...

Incas and Aztecs (25),
Art and Artists (27)

Medieval Europe

The Middle Ages fell between the time of the ancient Romans and the Renaissance, lasting from about AD 500 to 1450. By AD 500, the western parts of the Roman Empire had begun to break away. It was a time of endless battles, bloodshed and struggles for power. During this period, Christianity began spreading throughout Europe.

▲ **Joust**
Duels between armed knights, known as jousts, were common during the Middle Ages.

Quick Q's:

1. What was a castle?

A castle was the home and fortress of a lord or king. They had ramparts from which soldiers could attack the enemy if the castle was besieged. Many people besides the lord lived in it, including servants, soldiers, cooks, blacksmiths and falconers. Cows, horses, pigs and chickens were also kept there for food.

2. What did people wear?

Knights wore sleeveless coats decorated with their coat of arms. Rich men wore cloaks. Rich women wore tunics that reached to their ankles. Married women tied their hair in a bun and wore tight caps and nets over it. Unmarried women could leave their hair loose or braided.

Q How did the spread of Christianity affect medieval Europe?

A Although other religions existed in Europe, the Catholic Church ruled the lives of most people. It laid down its own laws, owned land and levied taxes. The Church was based in Rome and headed by the pope, but it also ruled from monasteries located in different parts of Europe. The Church was all-powerful, and people who openly spoke out against it risked being branded heretics and burned alive at the stake.

▼ **The power of religion**
The Catholic Church ruled every aspect of life in medieval Europe. It decided who lived where and how. It also controlled marriages and burials.

▼ Europe in the Middle Ages.

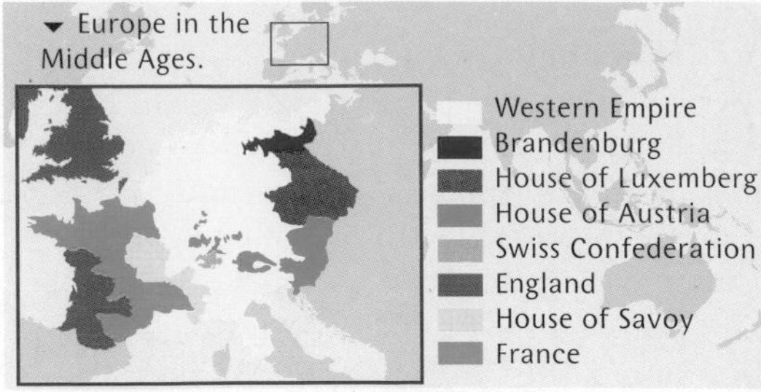

▸ **The keep**
Most forts had a high and strong keep to which defenders could retreat if necessary. Many of the keeps had secret tunnels for escape.

Keep

Q How were the various kingdoms governed?

A Much of western Europe was ruled by the feudal system. The king distributed land among noblemen in return for services and loyalty. Poor peasants rented this land from the nobles, and often paid them with livestock, eggs, firewood or wine. The nobles lived in a castle or a manor house.

Q How did the Crusades begin?

A The Crusades were a series of battles fought between Christians and Muslims. In AD 1095 Pope Urban encouraged Christians to free Jerusalem from Muslim rule. Several unorganized groups set off before they could be formed in to an army. Most of them died along the way. The main Crusaders left for Jerusalem in late 1096. They captured Jerusalem and other cities. This started a series of wars that went on for over 300 years, known as the Crusades.

Heroic thief

Robin Hood is a legendary hero whose story began in medieval England. He and his band of 140 men lived in Sherwood Forest in Nottinghamshire. They fought against the poverty and injustice of the feudal system by robbing the rich and giving what they stole to the poor.

Q Did King Arthur exist?

A Historians are not sure whether King Arthur was a legend or based on a real king. Some think he may have been a Celtic warrior who fought the invading Anglo-Saxons in the late fifth century. Stories about him have been popular since the twelfth century.

Q Who were the Vikings of Scandinavia?

A The Viking Age occurred between the eighth and eleventh centuries. The Vikings came from Denmark, Norway and Sweden. Most Vikings were farmers who were also great travelers and explorers. They traveled in winter when they could not farm. They were fierce warriors who attacked the coasts of Europe in their longboats, capturing new lands to farm. Many of these attacks were very violent and earned the Vikings a reputation for being barbaric. The Vikings settled in colonies in Scotland, Iceland, Greenland, Newfoundland in Canada, and many other places along the shores of the Atlantic Ocean.

Try these too...

Ancient Greece (12–13), Ancient Rome (14–15), Architecture (26), Art and Artists (27), World Religions (28–29)

▲ **Couple from the Middle Ages**
Rich people wore long and heavy cloaks.

▼ **Garbage disposal**
The habit of throwing garbage on to the street led to many diseases.

Q What was the Black Death?

A In the mid-fourteenth century, the bubonic plague broke out in Europe. It began as a disease of flea-infested rats, but quickly moved to people and spread like wildfire. It is likely that it was carried from the East along trade routes and by Crusaders returning to western Europe. It killed around 25 million people within five years. It was called the Black Death because of the black-colored boils that appeared on the victims' skin.

Medieval China and Japan

By about AD 500, the world was becoming more connected. Technology had improved, allowing people to travel more and learn from each other. With more trade and travel, religions started to spread. This was the period during which Buddhism spread in China and Japan.

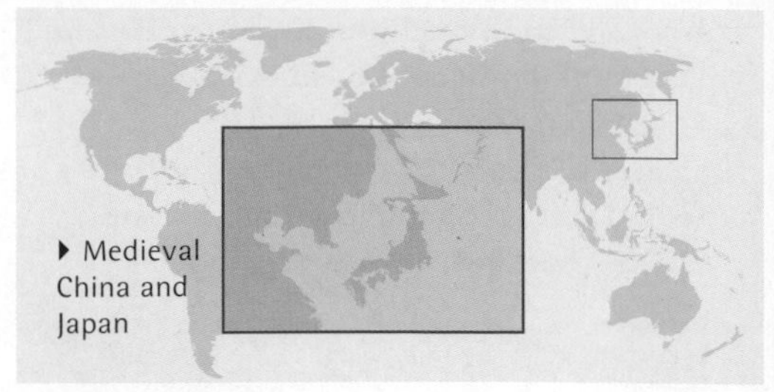

▸ Medieval China and Japan

Quick Q's:

1. What was the Silk Route?

The Silk Route was an important trade route that began in China and ran across Central Asia, all the way to Europe. Silk was the cloth worn by royalty in China. This land route was important until the early sixteenth century.

2. What is origami?

The Japanese perfected the art of folding paper into three-dimensional figures and shapes. Origami may have come to Japan with Buddhist monks from China. Others believe Origami is an art form that was developed in Japan. Only a few folds are used in Origami, but the folds can be combined in a variety of ways to make complicated designs. Most Origami designs begin with a square sheet. The two sides may be in two different colors. Usually, the paper is not cut.

Q Which was the first major dynasty to rule China during this era?

A The Han dynasty had a long rule from 206 BC to AD 220. This was enough time for a strong dynasty to bring most of modern China together. Under a long line of strong rulers, stability and peace spread. The Han dynasty saw the development of Chinese philosophy. This was also the time when a new religion came to China. Missionaries from India brought Buddhism, a religion that preached peace. Many Chinese people converted to Buddhism.

Q Why is the Tang dynasty famous?

A During the Sui dynasty (AD 589–618), cultural changes began in China. Then came the Tang period, between AD 618 and 907. This is known as the Golden Age of China. Learning and the fine arts developed like never before. When the young king Tang T'ai-tsung took over in 618, he made the government stable and strong. This encouraged agriculture and trade, and China grew prosperous. The arts flourished. Talented people did a lot to improve landscape painting, music, poetry, ceramics and metalwork. Sculpture became popular. Buddhist art was developed. Tang stone pagodas and paintings from the Dunhuang caves are fine examples of art from this age.

◂ **Folded paper**
Origami, the Japanese art of folding paper, uses a small number of different folds. They can be combined in a variety of intricate designs.

Q What were the major developments of this period?

A As early as AD 105, the Chinese knew how to make paper and how to print. They perfected printing and used wooden blocks to print books. Science was also prospering. China gave the world the compass. While Europe struggled to fight the plague, China, Korea and Japan were developing rapidly. However, some strange ideas also crept in.

◂ **Mongol emperor**
Genghis Khan (1162–1227) was the first of the great Mongols. He brought China, Tibet, Burma, Iran, Eastern Europe, and parts of Russia under Mongol control. In 1234, the Mongols had northern China in their grip. It took them some time to bring the rest of this vast country into their fold.

During the Sui dynasty, around AD 500, the emperor ordered that only the rich would wear colors and the common people would wear blue or black. During the Sung dynasty, around AD 1100, a painful sign of nobility was used. The feet of little girls were bound so tight that they never grew more than 7.6 centimeters (3 inches) long. The bandages broke the toes of girls as young as five years old. The toes bent under the feet. As women, they could barely walk. These lily feet were in fashion for over 1,000 years until they were banned in 1912.

◄ **Delicate work**
The artefacts made in medieval China were of porcelain stone. China clay was added in the eighteenth century. It increased the strength of the artefacts.

Q Why is the Ming dynasty so famous?

A The Mongols, who ruled China for 89 years, were overthrown by Hung-Wu in AD 1368. That marked the start of the Ming dynasty, which lasted until 1644. The Ming dynasty is remembered for making the administration strong, widespread and fair. Judges had to take a test to get a job. Chinese literature, art and philosophy reached new heights during Ming rule. Some of the best Chinese porcelain was manufactured at Jingdezhen. The yellow imperial bowls, red vases and highly decorated painted ceramics became popular. For the first time, both cotton and silk production did very well.

Q Who were the shoguns?

A Across the sea, Japan saw a long period of peace under the Seii Tai shogun or shoguns, military dictators who ruled from 1192 to 1867. The term means "barbarian-subduing generals." Minamoto Yoshinaka was the first modern shogun, who came to power after defeating the Taira dynasty. The shogun rulers had loyal warrior servants known as samurai. Samurai is from the Japanese word *saburau*, which means "to serve." Japan developed far slower than China because it was a group of islands, cut off from the mainland of Asia. It was only in AD 405 that the Japanese adopted a written language and even then they developed a writing system based on the pictorial alphabet of the Chinese.

Q What did the Chinese take to Japan?

A Around the fourth century, Chinese settlers taught the Japanese how to grow and weave silk. The Japanese wore hemp clothes before that. In the sixth century, Buddhism spread among the Japanese from China. Japanese art of this period includes wooden and bronze statues of Buddhist figures, landscape paintings and scroll paintings. The Japanese built magnificent pagodas. Literature developed. The Chinese also taught them a form of theater. The Japanese combined it with their own comic plays and created a new form, the *noh*. The Japanese learned about tea from the Chinese in the ninth century. They later developed a ceremony around it. The *Tale of Genji*, one of the earliest Japanese classics, dates to the eleventh century.

Try these too...

Ancient India and China (10–11), Architecture (26), Art and Artists (27), World Religions (28–29)

▲ **World heritage**
Built in stages between 1346 and 1601, Himeji Castle is one of the best examples of medieval Japanese architecture.

National dress

Kimono, in Japanese, means clothing. In recent years, it has come to mean a traditional Japanese robe. Kimonos came into fashion during the Heian period (794–1192). Before that, the Japanese wore separate upper and lower garments, or one-piece robes. In the Heian period, a new stitching technique led to the kimono. Cut in straight lines, these kimonos were suitable for all weather. As techniques improved, so did the kimono. They even became family heirlooms. The kimono was the most popular garment in Japan until about 50 years ago. Today, the kimono is only worn on special occasions like the tea ceremony.

Mughal India

In 1526, Babur, a Turk from central Asia, occupied Agra in northern India. He expanded his influence throughout the region and founded the Mughal Empire. The Mughal Empire continued until 1857.

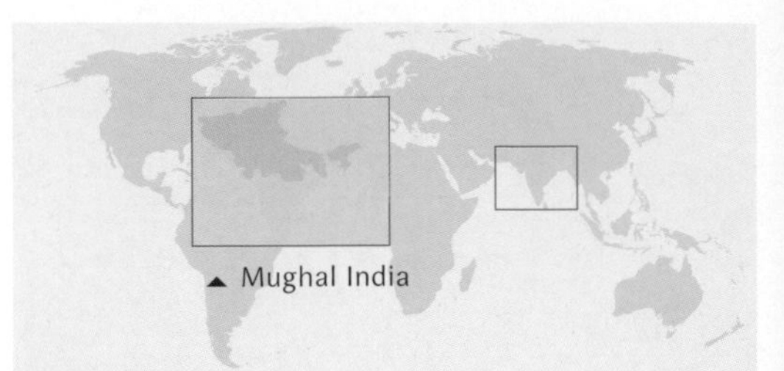
▲ Mughal India

▸ Inlay work
Inlay work on stone reached its height in Mughal India. It was used to decorate mosques, mausoleums and palaces.

Quick Q's:

1. What does Mughal mean?

Mughal comes from the Persian word for Mongol. The first Mughal Emperor Babur was from a Mongol family.

2. What is the Taj Mahal?

The Mughals loved architecture. They built complicated and intricately decorated mosques, tombs and strong forts at Agra and Delhi. They also studied the science of landscaping and created beautiful gardens. Shah Jehan built the Taj Mahal as a tomb for his beloved wife, Mumtaz Mahal.

3. Who were the *navratna*?

Navratna means nine jewels in the Hindi language. These were nine talented men in the court of Akbar. They were given special powers. They included Tansen the singer, Todar Mal the administrator, Abul Fazl, the emperor's chief advisor, and Maharaja Man Singh, Akbar's trusted general.

Q Who was Akbar?

A Babur's grandson Akbar was the greatest of the Mughal emperors. He expanded the empire to cover most of northern India. His reign brought peace and prosperity. Although Akbar could not read or write, he encouraged philosophers, poets, artists, architects and musicians. He died in 1605. His son Jehangir and Jehangir's son Shah Jehan enjoyed long and prosperous reigns. For the first time, the Mughals gained control of western India. Under Shah Jehan's son Aurangzeb the empire covered almost all of south Asia.

Q How did the Mughals keep the empire together?

A The Mughals had a central government. The emperor was supreme. The highest nobles were mostly central Asians, Persians, Afghans, Indian Muslims and Rajputs. The Mughals won over the powerful Hindu Rajputs partly through conquest, and partly by respecting their customs. Akbar married Joda Bai, a Rajput woman. He even tried to start a new religion that included elements of all existing faiths in India. No single group was allowed to become powerful enough to threaten the emperor. Tax was paid in cash, which was spent on creating new towns and markets. European traders visited Mughal India frequently and trade prospered.

▾ Poetry in stone
The Taj Mahal in Agra, India.

Incas and Aztecs

The Incas and the Aztecs ruled the last ancient empires of Latin America. The Incas expanded their kingdom in the twelfth century, and by the early sixteenth century, they had more land than any other people in South America. The Aztecs had their empire in Central America, in today's Mexico.

◂ The Inca empire

Try these too...

Ancient India and China (10–11), Ancient Americas (16), Native Americans (17–19)

Q What did the Incas do for a living?

A The Incas were good farmers, even though farming was difficult in the Andes mountains, where they lived. They carved terraced fields, where they grew corn, chilli peppers, beans, squash, peanuts, cassava, quinoa and potatoes. They knew how to irrigate their fields. They used tools like spades, clubs, hoes, sticks and foot ploughs. The Incas domesticated animals like the llama and alpaca for wool and to use as transport. They were good at construction and fitted gigantic stone pieces together without using mortar. They built bridges and tunnels through the mountains. They studied medicine and performed operations. They worshiped many gods and believed in heaven and hell. Of all the gods, the Sun God was the most important, and they built many temples in his honor. When an Inca king died, his body was mummified. People would offer the mummy food and consult it to solve problems. Ordinary people were also mummified, but they were buried.

Q What happened to the Incas?

A In 1531, a Spanish General named Francisco Pizarro invaded the Inca with only two hundred soldiers. He tricked the Inca ruler, Atahualpa, into meeting him in Cajamarca. Pizarro then kidnapped him and killed hundreds of his family and followers. Atahualpa was killed in 1533. Different Inca tribes did put up resistance for 30 years, but the Spanish defeated them. This ended the largest and richest South American empire.

Q Who were the Aztecs?

A The Aztec were the last tribe to arrive in Central America. In 1325, they founded the city of Mexico-Tenochtitlan. They built one of the strongest armies in the region. Between 1428 and 1521, they had the largest empire in Central America. The Aztec Empire fell in 1521, when they were defeated by the Spanish General Hernan Cortes.

◂ Spanish invader
Spanish General Francisco Pizzaro defeats the Incas in battle. The Incas had a large and disciplined army, but they could not hold out against the Spaniards.

▴ Terraced farming
Terraces on mountain slopes held soil and water and allowed the Incas to farm the slopes. The Incas developed new techniques to build the terraces.

A bridge made of grass

The Incas were good with their hands. They knew how to plait grass into strong rope. They built suspension bridges with this rope which they wove together (as shown here). Some bridges were 61 to 91 meters (200 to 300 feet) long. Although made of grass, they lasted several hundred years.

Architecture

Architecture is what goes in to designing a building. It can influence anything from a tool shed to a monument like the Taj Mahal. Architects also design buildings such as the Taipei 101 Tower in Taiwan, which stands 509 meters (1,670 feet) tall and was the tallest completed structure in the world in 2006.

Quick Q's:

1. Why is the Parthenon famous?

The Parthenon was a temple to the Greek goddess Athena. It was built between 447 and 433 BC and still stands at the Acropolis in Athens. Its decorative sculptures made of white marble make it an example of the best Grecian architecture.

2. What is Stonehenge?

Stonehenge, built between 3000 and 1500 BC, is the best known prehistoric stone structure in England. It is formed of tall standing stones, or megaliths, set in a circle within even older earthworks. It has been declared a World Heritage Site.

▲ Stones in a circle
Modern scholars believe Stonehenge was an ancient observatory, used for predicting phases of the Moon.

Q Have the earliest buildings lasted?

A The earliest buildings were of bark, leaves, mud and straw. They did not last long. But later, people began to build temples and palaces of stone. The earliest structures that we know of were built in about 9000 BC in the Neolithic or New Stone Age. These include the world's oldest stone temple, the Gobekli Tepe, in Turkey. Around 7000 BC the Sumerians, Assyrians and the Egyptians made huge improvements in building. Some of the most remarkable early buildings, including Sumerian *ziggurats* (temples) and the Egyptian pyramids, were made around 3000 BC. As people grew more confident in architecture, the buildings got bigger and more decorative.

Q What were medieval buildings like?

A With the spread of Christianity, some of the best medieval architecture was seen in churches. Churches were built in two styles: Romanesque and Gothic. The Romanesque style typically used brick vaults and rounded arches. Gothic churches like the Salisbury Cathedral in England and Notre Dame de Paris in France are tall churches with pointed-arch windows and doorways. They are supported by buttresses and they have beautiful stained-glass windows to let light in. During the Renaissance, architecture was inspired by the classical age of Greece and Rome.

▼ Building a cathedral
Stones unloaded by boats for the making of a cathedral were raised through a system of pulleys. They were dressed by expert stonemasons before being put in place.

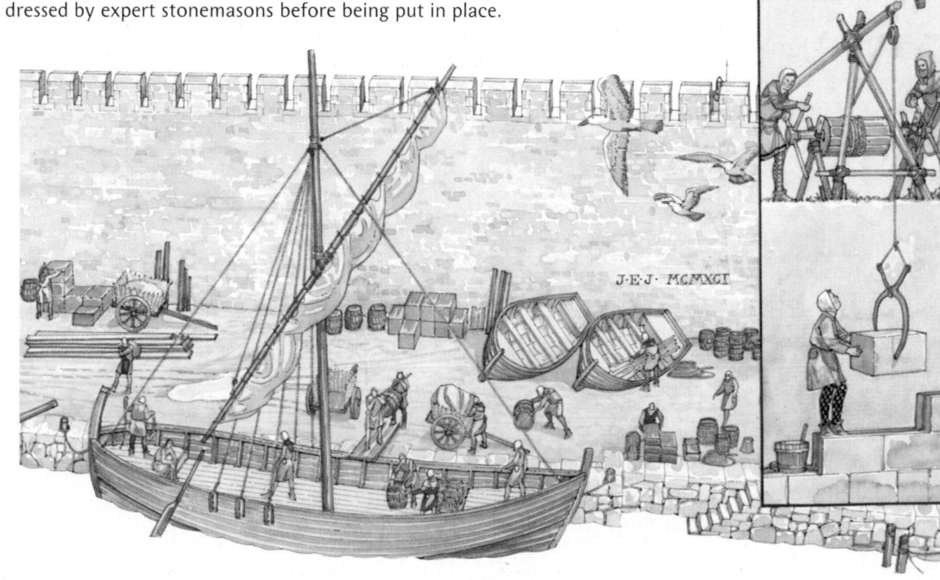

Art and Artists

Art is the way people represent themselves and the world visually. They do this by drawing, painting, sculpture and other means. The earliest art that we know of are rock and cave paintings which date back about 40,000 years. The artists used natural dyes extracted from plants and stones.

▲ **The ancestor of all artists**
A cave painting in Brazil shows life as it used to be. The painter used colors made from vegetable dyes.

Q What were the earliest paintings about?

A The earliest paintings were about things people did every day like hunting, and about the wild animals they saw. Horses, bison, deer and even human hands were drawn. These paintings were often made with pieces of colored stone. The painters were probably holy men or shamans. Some of these paintings were of such a high standard that they were believed to be fakes. When the Altamira caves in Spain were found and studied in the nineteenth century, many people believed the historians themselves had painted them. The first sculptures also date back to the prehistoric age. One of the most famous statues is the stone image of a woman, named Venus of Willendorf (Austria). It was carved 22,000 to 24,000 years ago.

Q Did different ancient civilizations have their own art?

A Each ancient civilization, including Egypt, Mesopotamia, China, Greece, Rome and India, had its unique art style. Art was used for worship, but it also came to be seen as a form of beauty. Paintings of Egyptian gods and goddesses covered the insides of pyramids. The Mesopotamians covered the walls of their temples with paintings. The Greeks studied the human body closely, and their paintings and sculptures include details of muscles and proportion. The Chinese were among the first to paint on paper and used painting to develop the script for the Chinese language. Indian artists were highly skilled at carving and painting on walls.

Q How was art important during the Middle Ages?

A Art and sculpture of the Middle Ages can be divided into the Romanesque period and the later Gothic period. The spread of Christianity meant that more churches were built. These churches were decorated with images from the Bible. To show their respect for God, painters used a lot of gold color, made out of real gold. While statues from the Romanesque period are still around, little of the fresco art survived. Gothic art gained ground gradually. Art was also used to decorate hand-written books.

Try these too...

Ancient Mesopotamia (8), Ancient Egypt (9), Ancient Greece (12–13), Ancient Rome (14–15), Medieval Europe (20–21), Mughal India (24)

The Renaissance

The Renaissance, which lasted from the fourteenth to the sixteenth century, was a highly creative period for artists and sculptors. Much of the inspiration came from the temples, paintings, and statues of ancient Greece and Rome. Renaissance artists believed in the importance of the human being. They explored the human form and captured scenes from things around them. They learned about perspective, or the importance of size and distance in a painting. They painted landscapes and developed new styles as well as new materials to paint with. The invention of oil painting meant that pictures lasted far longer without fading.

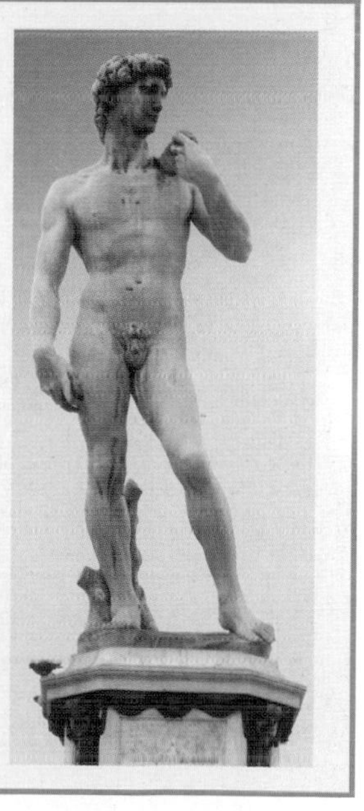

World Religions

Religion is a set of rules based on faith in a spiritual power. Every civilization has its religion. Religion can also mean faith in plants, animals, ancestors and spirits. Pantheism is the belief that there is something spiritual in everything around us. The word religion comes from the Latin noun religio, or rituals and faith. Most religions practiced today were started long ago.

▲ **Ancient Egyptian gods**
These gods were portrayed as half-human half-beast.

Quick Q's:

1. What is the meaning of Zoroastrianism?

Zoroastrianism is a religion founded in Persia around the sixth century BC by the prophet Zarathushtra. Arabs later banned the religion. Zoroastrians or Parsees fled to India. Zoroastrianism believes in one god, Ahura Mazda. Their holy book is the Avesta.

2. Who are the Amish?

The Amish are a Christian sect known for their shunning of modern technology. The Amish, who live in the United States and in Ontario (Canada), avoid the use of electricity and cars as far as possible. They do not join the military, nor do they take any money from any government. They place a high value on humility, and are strongly against pride.

Q What is Judaism?

A Judaism, the religion of the Jewish people, has about 15 million followers around the world. It began about 3,500 years ago in Palestine. Judaism is perhaps the earliest religion to preach belief in one god. The laws of God are known as the Ten Commandments, which God revealed to Moses on Mount Sinai. These laws are written in the Old Testament of the Bible. The Torah is the holy book of Judaism. This religion influenced later religions that began in the region, including Christianity, Islam and the more recent Baha'i faith. The Jewish temple is called a synagogue. Jewish people believe they should pray three times a day. Saturday or Shabbat is a day of rest and prayer, to remember that God rested on this day after creating the world in six days.

Q Did ancient Man believe in religion?

A There are signs that every ancient civilization believed in a higher power. The ancient Egyptians worshiped many gods like Anubis, Set, Osiris, Isis and Horus. Egyptian Kings, called pharaohs, were believed to be God's representatives on Earth. The ancient Egyptians were the first to prepare the dead for an after-life. They buried kings and commoners with many things they believed would be needed in the after-life. The ancient Mesopotamians, especially the Sumerians, had a strong belief in several gods who took human form.

However, they believed that these spirits had superhuman powers and so they could not be seen. Four of their main gods were An, the god of heaven; Ki, the goddess of earth; Enlil, the god of air; and Enki, the god of water.

Q Which is the oldest religion in the world still practiced?

A Hinduism began before 1500 BC. It grew from the four Vedas—religious texts written by scholars. The Vedas contain hymns and information about rituals. Hinduism believes that the world was created by Brahma, and is maintained by Vishnu. Any destruction in the world is ascribed to Shiva. The two major sects of Hinduism are Vaishnavism, or the path followed by the followers of Vishnu, and Shaivism, where Shiva is the main deity. Apart from Brahma, Vishnu and Shiva, the mother goddess, in her many forms, is worshiped as Shakti, or strength.

▲ **Hindu god**
The elephant-headed god Ganesha is one of the most popular of the Hindu deities. As in other ancient religions, Hindu gods are often depicted in various supernatural forms that are symbolic.

Q Who started Buddhism?

A Siddhartha Gautama was born in 563 BC. Troubled by sickness, sorrow and suffering, he left his palace to meditate or think about life. When he found the answers to his questions, he became known as the Buddha—Enlightened One. Buddhism is practiced in Nepal, India, China, Myanmar, Thailand, Japan, Korea and Sri Lanka, among others.

Q What is Christianity all about?

A Christianity is practiced in every continent where humans live. There are over 1.9 billion Christians. They follow the teachings of Jesus Christ, who lived about 2000 years ago. The New Testament of the Bible, the holy book of the Christians written after his crucifixion, details the life and teachings of Jesus.

▲ The headquarters of the Catholic Church
St Peter's basilica in the Vatican—the seat of the pope, who is the head of the Catholic Church.

Q When did Islam begin?

A The Prophet Muhammad founded Islam in the seventh century AD in Arabia. Islam is the second largest religion in the world. The holy book of Muslims is the Qur'an. Muslims believe that the Qur'an was revealed to Prophet Muhammad by God through the Angel Gabriel. Islam has one God. The word Islam means "peace" and "obedience to God."

▲ Shrine of the Báb
The tomb in Haifa, Israel, of the founder of Baha'ism. Started in the nineteenth century, it is the world's youngest religion.

▸ Old symbol
The menorah, the seven-branched candlestick, is one of the oldest symbols of Judaism. It was used in the Temple of Jerusalem.

Try these too...

Ancient Mesopotamia (8), Ancient Egypt (9), Ancient India and China (10–11), Native Americans (17–19), Medieval Europe (20–21)

On the calendar

Each religion sets aside certain days as important. For Christians, Christmas, or the day Christ was born, is celebrated on 25 December. Easter, the day Christ rose from the cross where he was crucified, is commemorated on a Sunday in the middle of April. For Muslims, Eid ul-Fitr marks the end of a month of fasting during Ramadan. The date is decided by the cycle of the Moon. Eid ul-Adha marks the end of haj, the pilgrimage to Mecca. Jews celebrate their new year as Rosh Hashanah, which they believe was the day the world was created. Yom Kippur is the day of praying for forgiveness for mistakes committed. Hindus celebrate several festivals. Diwali, or the Festival of Lights, celebrates the victory of good over evil. Dussehra celebrates the victory of Lord Rama in his battle against the demon king Ravana. Buddhists celebrate Buddha Purnima as the Buddha's birthday.

Index

Akkadians 8
Apache 18
aqueducts 15
architecture 12, 15, 23, 24, 26
armies 16, 20, 25
art 10, 12, 16, 18, 22, 23, 24, 27
Arthur, King 21
Assyrians 8, 26
Athens 12
Aztecs 25

Babylonians 8
baths 10, 15
Black Death 21, 22
boats 8, 11, 19
Buddhism 22, 23, 29
building 15, 16, 17, 18, 20, 23, 25, 26
burials 16, 17, 20, 25

calendars 16, 29
castles 20, 23
Catholic Church 20, 29
children 10, 13, 19, 22
China 10, 22–23, 27, 29
Christianity 20, 26, 27, 28, 29
churches and cathedrals 26, 27
cities 8, 10, 15, 16, 17, 20
city-states 12, 13, 14
clothing 10, 14, 19, 20, 21, 23
Colosseum 14
Confucius 11
crafts 10, 11, 22, 23
crime 18
Crusades 20, 21
cuneiform 8

death 9, 16, 17, 21, 28
democracy 12, 13
disease 18, 21
drainage systems 10, 15
drama 13, 23

education 13
Egypt, ancient 9, 26, 27, 28
Europe 20–21, 22
Europeans 16, 18, 24, 25

farming 8, 9, 10, 11, 16, 17, 18, 21, 22, 25
feasts 15
festivals 18
feudal system 20, 21
fishing 9, 10, 16, 17, 19

gods and goddesses 8, 12, 14, 16, 18, 25, 27, 28
Greece, ancient 12–13, 14, 26, 27

hieroglyphics 9
Hinduism 24, 28, 29
Homer 12
homes 10, 14, 16, 17, 18, 19
hunter-gatherers 17, 18
hunting 10, 11, 17, 18, 19, 27

igloos 18, 19
Incas 25
India 10, 24, 27, 28, 29
Indus Valley civilization 10
Inuit 18–19
Iroquois Confederacy 17
irrigation 8, 25
Islam 20, 24, 28, 29

Japan 22–23, 29
jewelry 9, 10, 16
Judaism 28, 29

kings 8, 9, 14, 16, 20, 25, 28

laws 12, 15, 20, 28
literature 23

Maya 16
medicine and healing 11, 18, 25
men 10, 13, 14, 15, 20
Mesoamerica 16, 25
Mesopotamia 8, 27, 28
metalwork 10, 11, 22
Middle Ages 20–21
Minoans 12
Mississippians 17
Mohenjo-Daro 10
monasteries 20
Mongols 22, 23, 24
Mughal Empire 24
mummies 9, 25

Native Americans 17–19
Navajo 18
Nile River 9
nobility 20, 22, 24
North America 17–19

Olmec 16
Olympic Games 13

palaces 16, 26
Parthenon 12, 26
peasants 20
Peloponnesian War 12
Persians 12
pharaohs 9, 28
pope 20, 29
pottery 10, 11, 12, 17
priests 10, 16, 18
pueblos 18
punishment 14, 20
pyramids 9, 16, 26, 27

religion 8, 9, 11, 16, 18, 20, 22, 24, 25, 27, 28–29
Renaissance 20, 26, 27
roads 10, 15
Robin Hood 21
Roman Republic and Empire 14, 20
Rome, ancient 14–15, 20, 26, 27
Rome, city of 14, 20

samurai 23
scholarship 22
shamans 18, 27
shoguns 23
silk 10, 11, 22, 23
Silk Route 22
slavery 13, 14
soldiers 14, 16, 20, 25
Sparta 12
sculpture 12, 16, 23, 27
Stonehenge 26
Sumerians 8, 26, 28

Taj Mahal 24, 26
taxes 20, 24
tea 10, 11, 23
technology 22
temples 8, 12, 16, 25, 26, 27, 28
tombs 16, 24
tools 16, 19, 25
trade 8, 10, 16, 21, 22, 24
transport 8, 25
travel 21, 22

Vikings 21

wars 8, 12, 13, 14, 18, 20
weapons 10, 11
weaving 10, 16
women 10, 13, 15, 20, 22
writing 8, 9, 10, 11, 15, 16, 23, 27

ziggurats8, 26
Zoroastrianism 28